Cool STUFF for

— for —

YOUR GARDEN

A Division of ABDO

ABDO
Publishing Company

PAM SCHEUNEMANN

visit us at www.abdopublishing.com

Published by ABDO Publishing Company, a division of ABDO, P.O. Box 398166,
Minneapolis, Minnesota 55439. Copyright © 2012 by Abdo Consulting Group,
Inc. International copyrights reserved in all countries. No part of this book
may be reproduced in any form without written permission from the publisher.
Checkerboard Library™ is a trademark and logo of ABDO Publishing Company.

Printed in the United States of America, North Mankato, Minnesota
052011
092011

 PRINTED ON RECYCLED PAPER

Design and Production: Mighty Media, Inc.
Series Editors: Katherine Hengel and Liz Salzmann
Photo Credits: Anders Hanson, Shutterstock

The following manufacturers/names appearing in this book are trademarks:
Americana® Multi-Purpose™ Sealer, Elmer's®, Liquid Nails® Perfect Glue™, Rapala®,
Scribbles®, Sharpie®, Thompson's® WaterSeal®

Library of Congress Cataloging-in-Publication Data
Scheunemann, Pam, 1955-
  Cool stuff for your garden : creative handmade projects for kids / Pam
Scheunemann.
     p. cm. -- (Cool stuff)
  Includes index.
  ISBN 978-1-61714-984-9
  1. Garden ornaments and furniture--Juvenile literature. 2. Gardening for
children--Juvenile literature. 3. Children's gardens--Juvenile literature. 4.
Creative activities and seat work--Juvenile literature. I. Title.
  SB473.5.S356 2011
  635--dc22
                        2011003501

CONTENTS

GREAT STUFF FOR
GARDENS

There is a lot of cool stuff that you can make for the garden. Some gardens actually have a theme! For example, one gardener might have **gnomes** and fairies. Another may have all farm animal stuff. You can choose whatever fits with your garden. Use the activities in this book as a starting point. Take a look at other people's gardens to get more ideas.

Permission & Safety

Be Prepared

- Always get **permission** before making any type of craft at home.

- Ask if you can use the tools and supplies needed.

- If you'd like to do something by yourself, say so. Just make sure you do it safely.

- Ask for help when necessary.

- Be careful when using knives, scissors or other sharp objects.

- Read the entire activity before you begin.

- Make sure you have all the tools and **materials** listed.

- Do you have enough time to complete the project?

- Keep your work area clean and organized.

- Follow the directions for each activity.

- Clean up after you are finished for the day.

TOOLS AND

SMOOTH ROCKS

CONCRETE
STEPPING-STONE

SMALL PEBBLES

ACRYLIC PAINT
AND SEALER

CHARMS

CERAMIC LETTERS

WIRE CUTTERS

SMALL FLAT-NOSE
PLIERS

PLANTS

SEA SPONGE

FOAM BRUSHES

CONCRETE SEALER
SPRAY

MATERIALS

GREEN SHEET MOSS

POTTING SOIL

BIRDHOUSE

CLEAR FISHING LINE

STENCILS

LARGE SPLIT RINGS

TERRA-COTTA SAUCER

TERRA-COTTA POT

LIQUID NAILS ADHESIVE

PUFFY PAINT

WATERPROOF WOOD GLUE

PRUNING SHEARS

MARKERS

STUFF YOU'LL NEED

SMOOTH ROCKS   PERMANENT MARKERS
NEWSPAPER   PUFFY PAINT
ACRYLIC PAINT   ACRYLIC SEALER
FOAM BRUSHES

1. Find a bunch of smooth rocks. You can use different-sized rocks for different types of markers. Fist-sized rocks can mark rows of vegetables. Smaller rocks can mark individual plants. Use a larger rock to make a sign for your garden. You could use your name or say something like, "Welcome to My Garden."

2. Wash the rocks to remove all dirt. Let them dry completely. Spread the rocks out on newspaper.

3. Paint each rock with a base color. Coat them entirely. Try different colors for different plants!

4. Use the permanent marker to write the letter outlines on the rocks.

5. Fill in the letters with puffy paint or acrylic paint. Let the paint dry completely.

6. Paint the rocks with acrylic sealer. Let them dry. Then put your rocks in your garden!

Great
ZEN GARDEN

10

STUFF YOU'LL NEED

TERRA-COTTA SAUCER
SAND
ROCKS
SMALL RAKE OR PLASTIC FORK

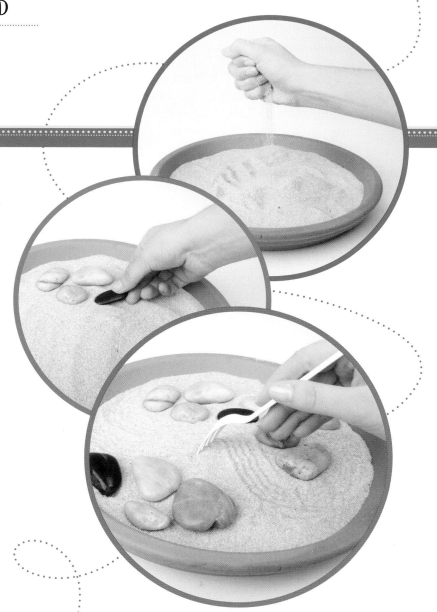

1. If you want to place your Zen garden in another garden, dig a hole the same size as the **terra-cotta** saucer. Place the saucer in the hole.

2. Fill the saucer about halfway with sand.

3. Place the rocks in the sand. You can pile them up or spread them around. It might work best to use only a few.

4. Here's the fun part! Use the rake or plastic fork to make cool patterns in the sand. Trace around a rock with the fork. Draw straight or wavy lines. Use your imagination!

5. If you like, add decorations such as flowers or twigs.

Ship-Shape
SHOE PLANTER

CHECK OUT THESE HIGH-STEPPING PLANTERS!

STUFF YOU'LL NEED

OLD SHOE OR BOOT
SMALL PEBBLES
POTTING SOIL
PLANTS

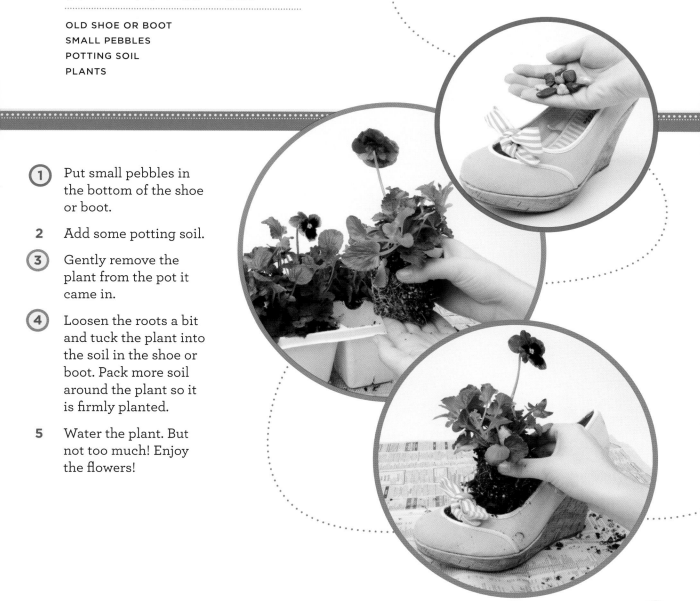

1. Put small pebbles in the bottom of the shoe or boot.

2. Add some potting soil.

3. Gently remove the plant from the pot it came in.

4. Loosen the roots a bit and tuck the plant into the soil in the shoe or boot. Pack more soil around the plant so it is firmly planted.

5. Water the plant. But not too much! Enjoy the flowers!

FAIRY HOUSE

HOME of the FAIRIES

STUFF YOU'LL NEED

NATURAL DECORATIVE ITEMS
UNPAINTED WOODEN BIRDHOUSE
ACRYLIC PAINT
FOAM BRUSHES

PERMANENT MARKER
SMALL PEBBLES
WATERPROOF WOOD GLUE
TWIGS

PRUNING SHEARS
GREEN SHEET MOSS
PINECONES
MEDIUM-SIZE STONE

1   Gather all the natural **materials** you can from outside. Find twigs and pebbles. Look for pieces of bark on the ground. Don't take any off of a live tree! Look for other materials such as nutshells or seeds. You can also use feathers, shells, or pinecones.

2   Paint the birdhouse. Use different colors for the sides, roof, and around the base of the house. Let the paint dry.

3   Use a permanent marker to draw windows on both sides and a door on the front.

4   Glue the pebbles around the base of the house. Start from the bottom and work up.

5. Make shutters out of twigs. Use a pruning **shears** to cut the twigs. Cut 12 twigs as long as the windows are high. Cut six twigs as long as the door is high. Glue the twigs together side-by-side in groups of three. Then glue shorter twigs across the top and the bottom of each group of three twigs.

6. Glue a shutter on each side of the doors and windows.

7. Spread out the green sheet moss. Cut two pieces a little bigger than the side of the roof. Use a foam brush to put a coat of glue on the roof. Put the moss on the glue. It should hang over the edges a little bit. This will give it a more natural look.

8. Find a spot in your garden for the fairy house. Make a fence out of pinecones and twigs.

9. Paint a sign for your fairy house on a smooth stone. It could say "Home of the Fairies." Or think up a special name for your magical fairy house!

TIP

*Find other things that will look cute with your fairy house. There are **miniature** birdhouses, furniture, and tools. Put a small plant in a tiny flowerpot. Make walking paths and play areas for the fairies!*

Beaded
WIND CHIME

STUFF YOU'LL NEED

CLEAR FISHING LINE
RULER
SCISSORS
CHARMS

GLASS BEADS, VARIOUS SIZES
LARGE SPLIT RING
KEY RING
CERAMIC LETTER

WIRE
WIRE CUTTERS
SMALL FLAT-NOSE PLIERS
PENCIL

(1) Cut a 36-inch (91 cm) piece of clear fishing line. Tie a charm to one end. Make several knots. Then tie a large knot about 2 inches (5 cm) up from the charm.

(2) String about 12 inches (30 cm) of beads on the line. Use a **variety** of sizes and colors. Tie a secure knot at the top of the beads.

(3) Wrap the line around the split ring. Tie a secure knot. The knot should be on the top side of the split ring.

4 Add smaller beads for about 4 more inches (10 cm). Tie a knot at the end of the beads.

5. Wrap the line around the key ring. Tie securely. Trim the extra line, but not too close to the knot.

6. Repeat steps 1 through 5 until you have five strings of beads. Space the lines evenly around the split ring.

7. Cut another 36-inch (91 cm) piece of clear fishing line. Tie it to the **ceramic** letter. Make a few knots.

8. Add beads to the line above the letter. There should be about 18 inches (46 cm) of beads. Tie a knot at the top of the beads.

9. Bring the end of the line through the split ring. Then wrap it around the key ring and tie a secure knot.

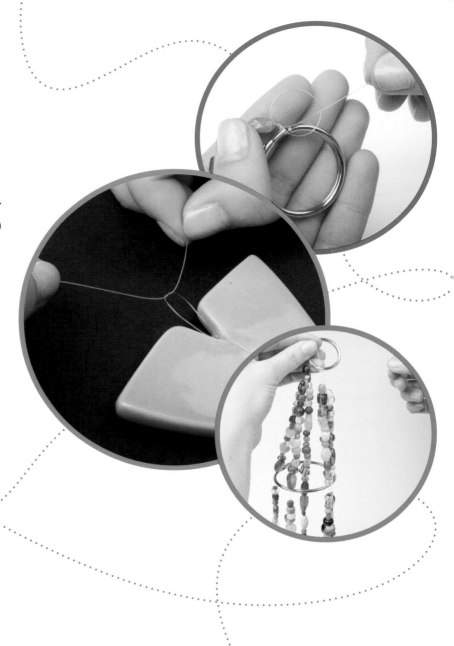

10. Cut a piece of wire about 18 inches (46 cm) long. Use the flat-nose pliers to bend one end into a **spiral**.

11. Wrap the wire around a pencil to make a loose **coil**.

12. Fill the coil with beads. Leave 2 inches (5 cm) free at the top of the coil.

13. Repeat steps 10 through 12 to make four more beaded coils.

14. Wrap the ends of the wires around the split ring. Put a wire coil between each pair of strings of beads. Wrap the wires a few times to make them secure.

15. Hang your wind chime and enjoy!

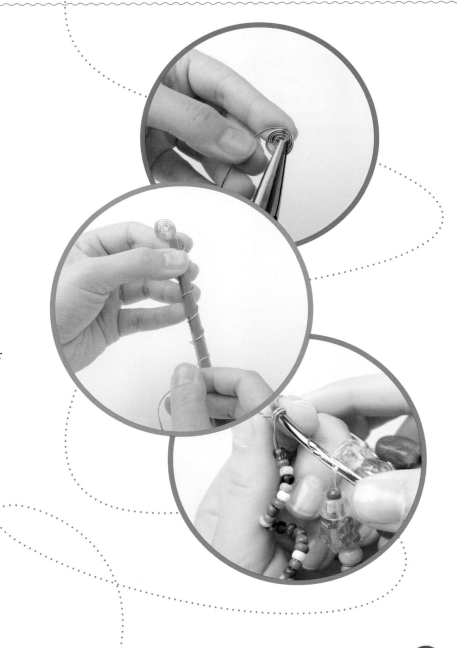

Super
STENCIL STEPS

STUFF YOU'LL NEED

NEWSPAPER
CONCRETE STEPPING-STONE
ACRYLIC PAINT
PAPER PLATES

FOAM PAINTBRUSHES
STENCIL
PAPER
TAPE

PAPER TOWEL
CLEAR CONCRETE SEALER SPRAY

Stencils are used to reproduce a **design**. A stencil is a sheet of plastic or cardboard that has a design cut out of it. The stencil is placed on a flat surface. Then paint is applied to the cut-out design. This makes a copy of the design on the surface under the stencil.

STENCILING TIPS

It is important to place the stencil exactly where you want the design to be. If it should be in the center of something, measure it to get the stencil in the right spot. Tape the stencil down so it doesn't move while you are painting.

Use a dry brush **technique** to paint the stencil. This means that the brush should not be soaking wet with paint. Put just a small amount of paint on the brush. Then dab the brush on a paper **towel** to remove any extra paint. That way the brush is almost dry. If any paint seeps under the edge of the stencil, the brush was too wet.

One method of stenciling is stippling. Stippling is tapping the brush on the stencil cut-outs, rather than brushing them. Do this until the whole design is filled in.

1. Spread newspaper over your work area. Set the stone on the newspaper. Put some paint on a paper plate. Use a foam paintbrush to paint the background color. Cover the whole top and sides of the stone. Let it dry completely before stenciling.

2. Practice stenciling on a piece of paper before you stencil your stepping-stone. Tape the stencil onto a piece of paper. Pour a small amount of paint on a paper plate. Lightly dip the stencil brush in the paint. Remove extra paint by dabbing it on a paper **towel**. Practice until you are happy with the results.

3. Now it's time to do the real thing! Rinse and dry your stencil. Start with the center **design**. Measure to find the center of the stone. Place the stencil so the design you want is in the center and tape it down.

4. Stencil the pattern by stippling. Let the paint dry before removing the stencil.

5. Next tape down the corner stencil. Stencil that pattern. Wait for it to dry and then remove the stencil. Repeat on the other three corners. Add any other stencil **designs** you want on your stone. Let the paint dry overnight.

6. Place the stepping stone on some newspaper outside. Have an adult help you with the concrete sealer spray. Apply the concrete sealer according to the directions on the can. Let it dry for 24 hours.

7. Find the perfect spot in the garden for your stepping-stone!

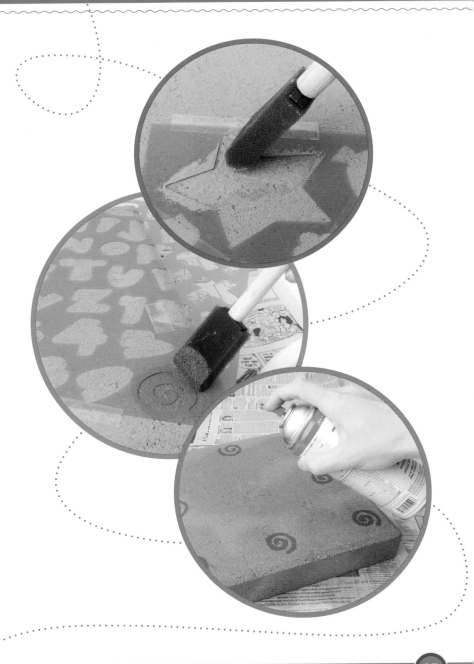

Double-Decker
BIRDBATH

THIS PROJECT IS ACTUALLY FOR THE BIRDS!

STUFF YOU'LL NEED

2 14-INCH (36 CM) TERRA-COTTA POTS

6-INCH (15 CM) TERRA-COTTA POT

16-INCH (41 CM) TERRA-COTTA SAUCER

8-INCH (20 CM) TERRA-COTTA SAUCER

CLOTH
ACRYLIC PAINT
PAPER PLATE
SEA SPONGE

FOAM BRUSHES
ACRYLIC SEALER
LIQUID NAILS ADHESIVE

1 Wipe all the pots and saucers with a damp cloth. Let them dry completely.

2 Paint the outsides of the pots with a base color. Paint the bottoms too.

3 Paint the two saucers a different color inside and out. Let them dry.

4 Paint the bottom of the inside of the saucers blue. Paint up the sides a little bit. This will make the water look blue.

5   Choose a different color paint than the base color. Put some on a paper plate. Dab the sea sponge into the paint. Don't get it too full of paint.

6   Use the sea sponge to dab paint below the rims of all three pots. Do not coat the whole surface with paint. Let the base color show through.

7   Repeat steps 5 and 6 with another color of paint.

8   Repeat steps 5 and 6 again with a third color of paint.

9   Touch up the rims with the base color if you got any specks on them. Let the paint dry completely.

TIP

Store the birdbath inside during the cold winter months.

10 Use a foam brush to apply the acrylic sealer to the painted areas. Let it dry and then put on a second coat. Let it dry completely.

11 Have an adult help you use the Liquid Nails **adhesive**. Glue the bottoms of the two large pots together. Glue the large saucer to the top pot. Glue the small pot upside down in the center of the large saucer. Glue the small saucer on the very top!

12 Put the birdbath in the garden and fill the saucers with water. Watch the birds come splash around in it!

CONCLUSION

The projects in this book are meant to inspire your creativity! Take some time to think about what you'd like in your garden. Do you have a garden theme or special colors? The more personal you make it, the more **unique** your garden will be.

Go a step further. Do some **research** on different things you can make for your garden. Try using different ideas or **materials**. See what you have around the house that you can use to make stuff. Be creative. The sky is the limit!

GLOSSARY

adhesive – something used to stick things to each other.

ceramic – made out of clay that is baked at high temperatures to become very hard.

coil – a spiral or a series of loops.

design – a decorative pattern.

gnome – a character from many folk legends that looks like a short, old man.

material – something that other things can be made of, such as fabric, plastic, or metal.

miniature – a small copy or model of something.

permission – when a person in charge says it's okay to do something.

research – the act of finding out more about something.

shears – large scissors that usually have a special purpose.

spiral – a pattern that winds in a circle.

technique – a method or style in which something is done.

terra-cotta – a hard, brownish-orange clay used to make pottery and tiles.

towel – a cloth or paper used for cleaning or drying.

unique – different, unusual, or special.

variety – a collection of different types of one thing. An assortment.

Web Sites

To learn more about cool stuff, visit ABDO Publishing Company on the World Wide Web at www.abdopublishing.com. Web sites about cool stuff are featured on our Book Links page. These links are routinely monitored and updated to provide the most current information available.

INDEX

DATE DUE

GAYLORD			PRINTED IN U.S.A.